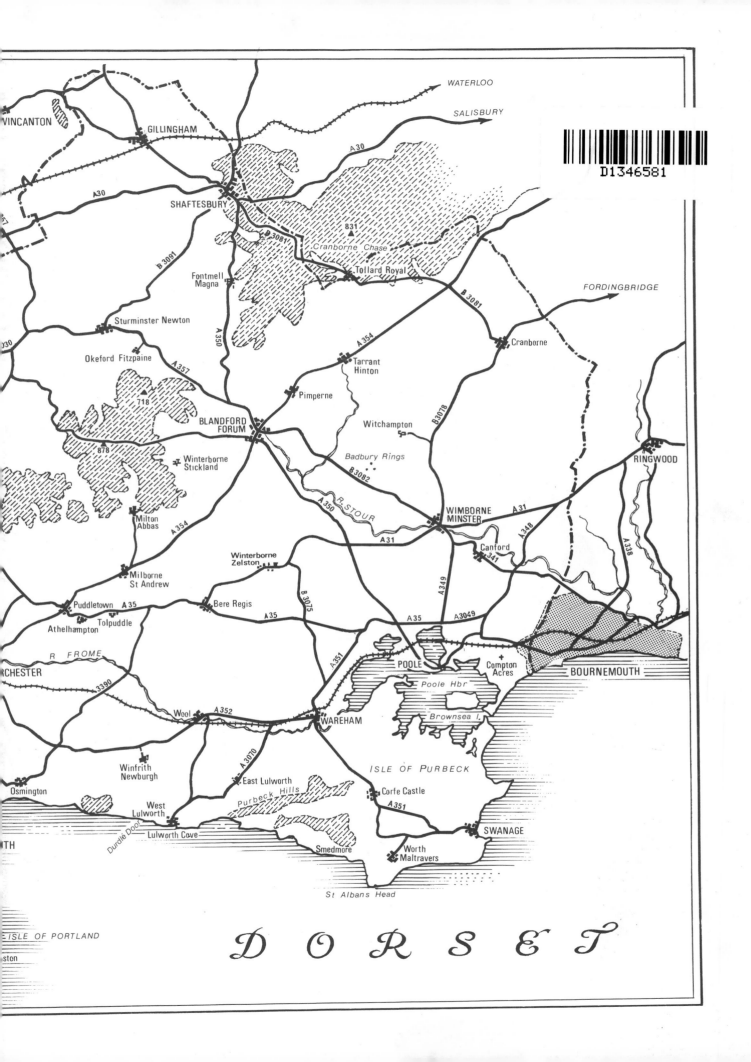

England in cameracolour
Dorset

England in cameracolour
Dorset

PHOTOGRAPHS BY ANDY WILLIAMS
TEXT BY MICHAEL H. C. BAKER

Town
& County
BOOKS

LONDON

First published 1983

ISBN 0 86364 009 5

Published by Town & County Books Ltd, Shepperton, Surrey;
and printed by Ian Allan Printing Ltd
at their works at Coombelands, Runnymede, England
Graphic reproduction by Southern Litho Services, Chertsey, Surrey

Introduction

What makes Dorset special? A very subjective question; easy enough for me to answer because it is where I live. I suppose one could reply that there are as many different answers as there are people who do indeed think that it is special. But that is really ducking the issue, and it should be possible to pin down certain features and characteristics which both residents and visitors would agree are the quintessential Dorset.

For our purposes Dorset is the county as it was before the boundary changes which took place on 1 April 1974. In many parts of England these were relatively insignificant; not so for Dorset. Until then there were only three towns with a population of over 10,000 — Weymouth, Dorchester and Poole. Now there were two more, Christchurch and Bournemouth. The latter was not merely the largest of them all, it actually claimed to be the largest resort in the country. My own, entirely subjective opinion, is that it is also very nearly the least interesting but that is neither here nor there. What is certain is that the character of Dorset was changed for good and all.

There was logic in putting the enormous Poole /Bournemouth /Christchurch conurbation (another claim was that it was the fastest growing urban area in Britain) under a single authority. But it has meant that Dorset, whilst still in terms of area very largely agricultural, is in terms of employment and business primarily dependent upon the holiday trade. Since the days of Jane Austen and George III it has been recognised that its coast has attractions for visitors and that its countryside is picturesque. Nevertheless it could never compete, nor wanted to, in terms of volume with the other south coast counties of Cornwall, Devon, Hampshire, Sussex and Kent. This was no reflection on its attractiveness but rather a consequence partly of the nature of its coastline which is in many places inaccessible, and also of poor road and rail communications. Of the 1,024 square miles which Dorset occupies only 37 of them are taken up by Bournemouth and Christchurch, yet of its population of 592,000 nearly one-third lives in that 37 square miles. No less than 82.4% of Bournemouth's working population is in service industry, which is largely concerned with catering for leisure, whether it be in the form of ice cream parlours, fortune-telling on the pier, or five star hotels and the Bournemouth Symphony Orchestra. A mere 0.1% is in agriculture, though just where this minute proportion finds employment is a bit of a mystery unless it be minding donkeys on the beach.

Elsewhere in the county it is a very different story. In the Blandford area 14.2% of the working population is employed in agriculture, 12.6% around Shaftesbury, 11.5% around Sherborne and 8.4% around Wareham. Even these figures may not seem particularly high, and it has to be admitted that they are slowly but steadily declining, but they are nevertheless impressive when set against the national average of just 1.7% which works on the land.

We have looked first at the seaside and then at the land, and it is reasonable to claim that it is these two aspects which are Dorset's chief attractions, followed perhaps by its remarkably long history of settlement. There are well over 150 known mesolithic sites the earliest going back to around 10,000BC. They are virtually all up on the Downs where no one — apart from shepherds and stranded hang glider pilots — has lived for many centuries, but as prehistoric man became more skilled and adventurous and moved down into the valleys so he established settlements which still exist today.

It may sound a bit obvious to say that Dorset is seaside and country — anyone can discover that merely by looking at the map. True, but nevertheless living as I do in Wareham which is within a mile of Poole Harbour and therefore very nearly seaside, one is strongly aware that southern Dorset is very much a sea-dominated landscape, whilst the north of the county is quite different and one of the most rural parts of all England. The towns up in the north, Beaminster, Sherborne, Sturminster Newton, Gillingham and Shaftesbury are deeply rooted in the countryside, and even if mechanisation, increased efficiency and low wages have greatly reduced the numbers of those officially recorded as in full-time agricultural employment, there are many more in these towns and elsewhere in the county whose livelihoods depend directly on farming.

Domesday lists four boroughs in Dorset — Wareham, Dorchester, Bridport and Shaftesbury, although curiously not Sherborne. Findings of flint tools indicate that Sherborne has been a settlement since the Old Stone Age, that is before 8000BC and the last Ice Age, although the ice did not reach as far south as Dorset. There have been several discoveries of Roman habitation in or close to the town and the consecration of Aldhelm as its first bishop in 705AD ensured Sherborne's pre-eminence in the history of Christianity in the county, a position it has retained to the present day. St Aldhelm, a monk and a member of the royal family of Wessex, is almost the first character to emerge from the anonymity of the Dark Ages. He was greatly loved and the story of his life has come down to us, written by a fellow Benedictine monk, William of Malmesbury. The unique St Aldhelm's Chapel looks out from the cliffs on the edge of Weymouth Bay towards France. William tells us that Aldhelm had a church built close by whilst waiting at Wareham to set sail for Rome. One would like to think that this is the one — it is less than 10 miles from Wareham to St Aldhelm's Head — but there is no firm evidence to suggest the chapel goes back quite that far. However it is certainly possible that the oldest parts of Sherborne Abbey are contemporary with Aldhelm. Of equal antiquity, at least in its founding if not, perhaps, in its fabric is Wimborne Minster, which began as a convent and a monastery. King Etheldred, elder brother and predecessor of the great Alfred, was buried here in 871.

The establishment of the Christian church was, quite apart from its religious impact, an enormous step forward in the laying down of a settled order in Dorset. Clergy were appointed to districts, preaching at first in the open air — in winter as well as summer one supposes — beside stone crosses, a few of which remain, later in churches. Two other early Christian sites must be recorded, Shaftesbury the principal exception to the rule that Dorset people do not live on the heights anymore where a minster church was founded by King Alfred, and Wareham where another Saxon minster was virtually destroyed in 1841 in a fit of rebuilding zeal to which the Victorians were prone.

These historic towns certainly receive their visitors today but in inverse proportion to their distance from the sea. No one would really call Shaftesbury and Sherborne tourist centres, which probably doesn't bother anyone who lives there, for they are delightful, easy-going although not sleepy towns. Sherborne, despite being on the main London to Exeter road and railway routes has never developed any industry to speak off — Yeovil, four miles away across the Somerset border has taken on this role — nor, not surprisingly has 700ft high Shaftesbury. A place we haven't mentioned so far is the county town of Dorchester. This was the heart of Roman Dorset, Durnovaria, which stood on the road from London to Exeter. The most accessible Roman remains within the county are to be found in or close to Dorchester. The complete foundations of a town house are preserved beside the disgracefully ugly County Hall, completed in 1955 although the rotunda, the only internal section with any claim to distinction is pure 1930s Odeon style. Dorchester market, situated between the west and south stations and overlooked by the pungently powerful Eldridge Pope brewery can sometimes seem pure Thomas Hardy. No matter that much of what is on offer is gaudy plastic, it would have been gaudy lithographed tinplate in Hardy's time. The patter of the stallholders and their nomadic way of life, moving on from one West Country market to another, the renewal of acquaintanceships, the meeting of friends, the whole feel of carnival conjure up a scene from one of the great man's novels. Michael Henchard, the Mayor of Casterbridge was reunited with his wife at Maumbury Rings, across the road from the market. Maumbury is a perfectly preserved Roman amphitheatre, once capable of seating over 10,000 spectators and in later days until just over 200 years ago the site of public hangings. Immediately north-west of Dorchester, above the tunnel where the railway line to Yeovil emerges is Poundbury Camp, an Iron Age hill fort, whilst to the south incongruously approached through a modern housing estate is Maiden Castle.

This enormous Neolithic camp is one of the most spectacular pre-historic sites in all of Britain and quite, to my mind, without equal in Dorset. It needs the minimum of imagination when walking along the tops of the high banks, whether it be on a clear summer's day with views across half the county, on a damp, misty February morning, or when the autumn winds are howling, to conjure up visions of Neolithic men of 5,000 years ago, perhaps peacefully if warily, shaping flints, or later adding further ramparts, though goodness knows how such civil engineering feats were achieved, or its storming and capture by the Romans after a fierce battle when many of the defendants were killed. Their remains, and those of earlier inhabitants, including women and children, have been excavated; one was found with an iron bolt buried in his skull.

A few miles west of Maiden Castle on the summit of Blackdown Hill and visible from most of the county and beyond is Hardy's Monument. Not, as one might suppose, anything to do with Thomas the writer, but Thomas the admiral, the one who may or may not have been asked to kiss the dying Nelson. After his retirement he used to come up here and look out across Weymouth and the naval base of Portland to the Channel. Portland is a bleak, fascinating lump of stone, Weymouth a resort I warm to as readily as I turn away from Bournemouth.

Weymouth has something for everyone. The beach is almost entirely sand, fine and clean — usually — and very safe for bathing. A great many day trippers come to Weymouth for its magnificent beach, as do those on a week or fortnight's holiday, mainly from South Wales, the Bristol area, the Midlands and north-west England. Weymouth is not really in the Blackpool or Southend league, although it has a funfair and cheap and cheerful shops along the promenade in between the hotels patronised both in the past and the present by royalty (Prince Charles has stayed more than once in a Weymouth hotel whilst visiting Portland naval base) and these give it the vitality and vulgarity necessary to round off its character. Also on the promenade are two splendidly garish ornaments, a statue of George III complete with regalia all painted in the most glorious technicolour and an ornate light-bulb festooned clock tower celebrating one of Queen Victoria's many jubilees. But Weymouth is also a port, quite a large one serving both the Channel Islands and France as well as a fishing fleet. Whilst there is absolutely none of the uncontrolled industrial sprawl typical of many modern dock areas there are lots of interesting narrow streets full of neat Georgian and older buildings usually found only in the more ancient and no longer commercially active ports. Weymouth is also a venue for international yacht meetings, and there are plans to extend these and attract more business to the town. But it would be a pity if this caused Weymouth to become trendy and self-conscious, for it is neither at present.

The busiest cargo port in Dorset is Poole. Many Poole merchants made their fortunes and established the town's prosperity in the Newfoundland trade. Today the chief trade is with Cherbourg by way of the distinctive grey and yellow roll-on-roll-off lorry ferries. Cars are also imported and parked by the hundred on reclaimed land around the edge of the harbour whilst steel forms an important rail traffic. When I first knew Poole it was a scruffy, run-down place, but as this was in the last year of World War 2 it had every right to be. Since then it has been vastly re-developed and improved — although not everyone thinks so. It has a very fine arts centre, the remaining 18th century merchant venturers' houses have been superbly restored, whilst its museums are an example to all.

The years since World War 2, when the Dorset beaches were used first as a training ground and later a launching site for the Normandy landings — it seemed to me in 1944 that half the American Army was billeted in Bournemouth — have seen more and more visitors coming to the county. There are still areas on the heathlands around Bovington and T. E. Lawrence's cottage at Clouds Hill and stretching past Wool to Lulworth and the coast which the Army uses as firing ranges where visitors are forbidden or severely restricted, although ironically this has helped preserve otherwise threatened wildlife except where a shell actually lands in the middle of it and blows it to pieces.

Dorset needs visitors, both for its prosperity — I wouldn't say unemployment is unknown here but it is a different world from the depressed Britain north of the Home Counties — and also to hasten the end of the rural insularity which meant, and here and there still means, amongst other things a good deal too much interbreeding, illiteracy and poverty. Unfortunately visitors can also mean caravan-sites obliterating beauty sites, police signs at Wareham announcing that no more traffic can be allowed on to the Isle of Purbeck, and the chief constable deciding to issue his men with riot shields. Never mind that the most likely use for the latter is when the old ladies in the 'Bide-A-Wee' tea rooms at Charmouth get out of hand, for crime, certainly outside Bournemouth is conspicuous chiefly by its absence.

Weymouth would be a poorer place without its donkeys, Punch and Judy and sand sculptor, Swanage without its Victorian hotels and boarding houses and its steam railway run to a considerable degree and supported by retired ex-Londoners and others originally from out of the county, Lyme Regis without the fame brought by Jane Austen and John Fouldes, and the vast numbers of school parties which come all the year round to study Dorset's unique geology. The Coastal Path, opened ten years ago, is greatly appreciated by local people but surely would not have happened had it not been for the ever increasing number of visitors wanting to walk the spectacular cliff tops from Lyme to Old Harry.

If there is a threat to Dorset's rural and coastal beauties it is not tourism but the search for energy. Very little of the once extensive heathland lasted into the second half of this century and a good deal that did disappeared when the Atomic Energy Research Establishment was built on Winfrith Heath. Now another power station with enormous cooling towers is threatened which would effectively destroy a unique, precious and beautiful piece of countryside. In the Isle of Purbeck under more heathland and stretching out into the largest natural harbour in the northern hemisphere oil has been discovered and is now being pumped out at a rate equivalent to that of a North Sea rig. Britain as a nation needs oil and — perhaps — nuclear energy. It is ironic that a county for so long regarded as a rural backwater should in the 1980s find itself at the centre of the essentially modern energy debate.

M. H. C. Baker,
Wareham, 1983

Wimborne Blandford and Wimborne might almost be regarded as twins. Set in the Stour Valley and of similar size and antiquity they are both full of handsome buildings, the chief of which is the parish church, although in the case of Wimborne this is actually a minster. Even in these days of recession Wimborne has a prosperous air with a recently completed shopping development in the centre of the town and a carefully designed residential one close by. A by-pass, opened in 1981, has done much to relieve the once fierce congestion in the narrow main streets. Ribbon development and the northward expansion of the suburbs of Poole means that there is precious little countryside to the south and east separating Wimborne from the Poole/ Bournemouth/Christchurch connurbation. To the north and west, however, are lush, well-watered meadows and extensive heath and woodlands.

8

Wimborne Minster A place of worship at least since 705AD and pretty certainly the site of a Roman temple, Wimborne Minster — the nave is seen here — is very largely Norman. Despite 19th century restoration by Wyatt and Pearson the nave itself is almost pure 12th century, at least as far as the clerestory. There are some who do not think very highly of the Minster's exterior. It is, admittedly rather grey and heavy with its two, but certainly not twin towers, but for all that the mere presence of such a venerable building lends the town an air of distinction. And there can be no dispute that the interior, and particularly the nave, is very fine.

10

Compton Acres Like the area in which it is set Compton Acres has changed virtually out of all recognition since the early years of this century when it was created. Then the heathland on the Bournemouth side of Poole Harbour was an uninhabited, undeveloped expanse, beautiful in its way with superb views across the Purbeck Hills. Compton Acres house was built in 1914 and the creation of the 33-acre garden began shortly after World War 1 ended. Development was also taking place elsewhere on the heath, the beginning of the boom which resulted in the building of the palatial villas which now cover it. It took practically all the time between the two world wars for the gardens to reach maturity. They have been further developed and altered since their reopening in 1952 and are now visited by some 300,000 people each year. Much of the gardens has been carefully designed to allow wheelchairs and prams and children's buggies to move around amongst the gorgeous blooms, shrubs, trees and set pieces and which are open every day from April to October.

Looking down Church Street to the Guildhall, Poole There was a time in the years immediately after World War 2 when Poole, and particularly the area around the quayside wore a very run-down air. The war had taken its toll, much re-investment was needed and there were few visitors. But in the 1970s there was a transformation. Some of the very handsome Georgian houses in Church Street, close to the quay, were rehabilitated and any new building necessary was carefully designed to fit in with its surroundings. Part of the narrow streets was pedestrianised and elsewhere parking restrictions were imposed which effectively removed cars and returned the area to walkers. The Guildhall, one of the finest of Poole's Georgian buildings, with its distinctive flights of steps is now a museum illustrating the civic and social life of the town in the 18th and 19th centuries.

The Custom House, Poole One of the brightest jewels in the rehabilitation of Poole is its museum service. Using superb architectural settings it has displayed the many and varied treasures in its care in a most accessible and attractive manner. Beside the handsome red brick Georgian Custom House on the quay are the Town Cellars which are now the Maritime Museum. Poole has long been the principal port in Dorset, taking over this position from Wareham at the end of the 12th century. One of its chief exports was wool and the 15th century stone Town Cellars were alternatively known as the Wool House, for here the wool was stored before being put aboard ship. A much later warehouse, dating from the Newfoundland trade of the 17th and 18th centuries is next door. The Custom House was often used for storing contraband confiscated by the revenue men; on one infamous occasion the smugglers descended en masse on the Custom House, overpowered the handful of defenders and retrieved their haul.

16

Wareham Usually regarded as the gateway to the Purbecks, Wareham is a popular place for yachtsmen. (Strictly speaking the so-called Isle of Purbeck begins on the opposite bank of the River Frome from the quay seen here.) It is nevertheless possible to live, like I do, in the town without owning anything which floats. Wareham was once the chief port in the county and within living memory boats for the clay traffic, which still flourishes, were built on the banks of the Frome, but narrowness and lack of depth of the Wareham Channel saw the transfer of commercial traffic to Poole many centuries ago. That great writer of boys' sea stories in the 30s, Percy F. Westerman, used to live on a houseboat at Wareham, and, according to those who remember it, a pretty ramshackle, far from shipshape affair it was at least in later years. The River Frome marks the southern boundary of the town, the other three sides being formed by grass covered earth ramparts of Saxon origin and the most perfectly preserved in the land. The ancient Saxon church of St Martin, above the north walls and looking across Wareham's other river, the Piddle, contains Eric Kennington's handsome effigy of T. E. Lawrence who was killed at nearby Bovington. The town museum is a must for anyone interested in this extraordinary man. Wareham is full of little narrow streets lined with handsome cottages and houses. A fine place to live.

18

Corfe Castle 'Corfe Castle's not real, it's only there for the tourists.' Thus commented a headteacher from another part of Dorset when discussing Corfe Castle village. It was an understandable remark, for, nestling beneath the dramatic ruins of the castle it has an air of such picturesque, romantic perfection that would do justice to a film set. It is a quality it shares with Rye, Bath, Howarth, St Ives, Culross and the like and has, inevitably, been the setting for a number of films. But for the people who live there, and especially the children, Corfe Castle is an everyday reality, even if there are rather more souvenir shops, double yellow lines, car parks and coach parties than most Dorset villages boast. Some sort of fortification probably existed as long ago as the 9th century when the Danes destroyed Wareham, five miles to the north-west, but the great stone castle was begun in the next century by King Edgar. It was Cromwell's men, after a siege which succeeded only through treachery, who reduced it to its present state. In 1978, to commemorate the 1,000 anniversary of the death of King Edward the Martyr, a production of *Twelfth Night*, directed by Keith Martin, was performed in the ruins, a magical experience.

Swanage The pale grey Purbeck stone of the old cottages and the parish church surrounding the Mill Pond in Swanage looks its best in the summer sunshine. Swanage's history as a port for the stone traffic from the many quarries in the vicinity goes back to Roman times, but it owes its present role as one of the most delightful South Coast resorts chiefly to two men, John Mowlem and his nephew George Burt. They made their fortunes in the mid-19th century shipping stone to London, but they were also great benefactors of their native town. One of its most extraordinary buildings is their home, Purbeck House, just across the road from the Mill Pond, built in the style of a Scottish castle and today beautifully kept by the nuns of the Order of Mercy. The extensive gardens contain many relics from the Great Exhibition of 1851 and the fete held by the Sisters each summer in aid of their school is one of the highlights of the town's social calendar. Superbly set around the bay bounded by the Old Harry Rocks to the east and Peveril Point to the west, Swanage is still essentially Victorian in character with its bandstand, steam railway, neo-Gothic Durlston Castle, handsome villas and a plethora of delicate promenade ironwork tracery.

Man o' War and St Oswald Bays, West Lulworth These two bays between Lulworth Cove and Durdle Dor offer some of the best swimming on the Dorset coast which in many places is difficult of access. The rock strata here is contorted and heavily folded as is evident from the varying cliff colours. It is also of varying hardness and the hungry sea has consumed the softer rocks leaving offshore reefs like that visible here. This picture was taken on a calm summer's day but in winter the sea and the sharp toothed rocks can be ferocious and pitiless. The coast abounds with legends of shipwreck and the title 'Man o' War' tells its own story.

Worth Matravers This charming village is very much at the end of the road. Indeed as you come over the hill from the Kingston-Langton Matravers road you might well feel a sharpish application of the brakes advisable in order to avoid shooting right through the village and over the cliffs into the sea. Deep in the heart of the Purbeck quarries, the houses, the cottages and the church in Worth are naturally enough almost exclusively stone built. It is a pretty village; the country around is hardly that, rather bleak and windswept but magnificent too. A walk of a mile and a half brings one to St Aldelm's Head and its square, 12th century Norman chapel. I've stood here beside the coastguards' lookout on a mild autumn afternoon with the sun dodging in and out of the clouds and the air so keen and the light so bright it seemed eminently possible that one ought to be able to look beyond the supertankers travelling up the English Channel and see the coast of France. On such a day Worth Matravers, instead of seeming the end of Dorset has more the feel of the beginning of Europe.

26

Smedmore, near Kimmeridge Smedmore is set in wild, remote countryside with splendid views across the sea. It was built in the early 17th century by a member of the ancient Dorset family of Clavell. It was the Clavells who had the harbour at Kimmeridge, just down the hill from Smedmore, constructed — not for the benefit of local fishermen who are now its principal customers, but in the hope that it would become a proper commercial port. The Romans had made use of the shale found in the cliffs and in the 17th century Sir William Clavell hoped to make his fortune out of it. Attempts were made to make glass and lamp oil but without much success, and Sir William went bankrupt. Some 40 years ago a writer remarked rather smugly that he could 'hardly be sorry'; Sir William's ghost must be smiling to itself for it has had the last laugh. The nodding donkey on the cliffs at Kimmeridge is witness to the Purbeck oil boom which began here in the early 1970s and now constitutes the largest onshore oil field in the British Isles. Smedmore House is today essentially 18th century, the Wren style front seen here having been added by Edward Clavell around 1700.

Sunset over The Channel, from the cliffs above Lulworth Cove Away on the horizon to the west looms the Isle of Portland. The guide to the Dorset Coast Path describes the walk along the cliffs here as 'a crash-course in geology'. At any time of the year parties of school and college students can be seen at work. The deep, almost completely circular shape of Lulworth Cove has been formed by the sea breaking the Purbeck and Portland limestone and the scooping out the softer clays and sandstones beyond. The rock faces are far from stable in places — a teacher and three pupils from a Surrey school were killed by falling rocks eight years ago — and the public should pay strict regard to the warning notices. If they do there is no danger and each year tens of thousands avail themselves of the glorious views from the cliffs and the beaches.

Lulworth Cove One of a series of coves scalloped out by the sea along this section of coast and Lulworth is very much the most famous. It became popular towards the latter part of the 19th century with holidaymakers who came to wonder at its remarkable shape. Paddle steamers from Bournemouth, Poole, Swanage and Weymouth called regularly, although there is no quay and passengers had to disembark by way of rickety landing stages.

It is still possible to take a boat trip to Lulworth from Weymouth, at least in summer, but almost everyone now arrives by car. And how they pour in! I've never been quite sure what the attraction is. Lulworth Cove is a pleasant spot, especially out of season, an ideal centre for walkers and for skin divers and geologists, but there's no beach to speak of and nothing to occupy small children. Yet at the height of summer on a sunny day the enormous car park, very nearly as large as the Cove itself, is packed with family cars, row upon row,
hundred upon hundred.

Winterborne Zelston A charming corner of rural Dorset just off the main Wimborne to Dorchester road, this tiny village is one of the county's many 'Winterbornes'. The name comes from the old English for 'an intermittent stream' or 'a stream dry except in winter'. The river here, however, is rather more permanent and drains into the River Stour on its way to the sea at Christchurch and gives its name to many other villages in its valley. The second name — Zelston — is probably the name of the family that held the manor early in the hamlet's history c.1350 — possibly the Zeals. A neighbouring village, Winterborne Kingston, for example was held by the king in 1086.

The church seen here, St Mary's has a Perpendicular tower, c.1350-1530 made of stone but the rest of the church is flint and brown stone dating from 1865-6.

Woolbridge Manor, Wool Of all the locations associated with the characters created by Thomas Hardy Woolbridge Manor is perhaps the most poignant. It was here that Tess of the D'Urbervilles stayed on her flight to Salisbury Plain. D'Urberville and its derivatives was, and is, a real Dorset name encountered to this day in this part of the county. The handsome stone manor house dates from the 17th century. The five arch bridge beside it is a hundred years older. The road which passes over the River Frome has been by-passed in recent years, of necessity, for tanks and much other heavy military traffic travels this way from nearby Bovington Camp. The village of Wool, south of the manor is, apart from the modern Roman Catholic church, unimpressive when seen from the railway and the main road, but turns out to be much more interesting on further exploration. Ducks paddle about the stream which flows through the centre of the village, on either side are pretty thatched cottages, and a couple of beautifully converted barns. The name itself has nothing to do with sheep, despite the thousands which inhabit the fields around, but is thought to derive from an Anglo-Saxon chief, Welle, who once held sway here.

36

Winfrith Newburgh This is a most interesting village, not least because although it lies on one of the roads leading to Lulworth Cove it is not really on the tourist trail and is therefore distinctly unselfconscious. It has some charming whitewashed thatched cottages such as this, but other rather less picturesque but nevertheless well-cared for homes which do little to detract from the character of the village. It also has a trail, put together by the children of the local school with the help of the former teacher centre leader and largely inspired by David Bridges, clerk to the parish council and a tireless worker in the cause of conservation both in the village and on Winfrith Heath, a precious but threatened remnant of the once extensive Dorset heathland. Gustav Holst was inspired to write his suite *Edgon Heath* whilst walking here with his friend Thomas Hardy. Apparently featureless to the casual observer the Heath in fact is a precious breeding ground for such rare plants as marsh gentian, bog St John's wort and several varieties of orchids. Looming over the Heath a mile and a half from the village is the Atomic Energy Research Establishment. This is the most important and controversial development in Dorset since World War 2.

Durdle Dor A view looking across the sweep of the beach from Swyre Head. The curious arch is, like many of the features of this dramatic coastline, a result of the erosion of softer rocks, leaving the harder ones exposed. The beach is a suntrap in summer, and despite its relatively difficult access by way of a steep, narrow cliff path, it receives plenty of visitors. Entry is from a turning off the Weymouth to Lulworth road and through a large and inevitable caravan site. But the camp is some way back from the cliffs and invisible from the sea. The only piece of commercialisation close to the beach is a lone, innoffensive portable ice cream kiosk, the beach itself being completely undeveloped.

George III, carved in the chalk downs at Osmington Cut in 1808 by soldiers stationed at Weymouth to counter the threat from Napoleon, the 325ft high, 280ft long figure is a spectacular landmark dominating the A353 road as it sweeps down the last hill into Weymouth. During fine, dry weather when the white chalk shows up clearly the figure can be seen from a considerable distance out to sea. The walk up to it is hard work but well worth the effort both for the sense of achievement and the view across Weymouth Bay to Portland and the English Channel. Part of the route from Preston village is by way of ancient trackways which were once of rather more than local significance. The story goes that when King George saw his likeness he was far from pleased because it faced away from Weymouth. He never visited the town again; possibly his loss was the greater.

42

The Smugglers Inn, Osmington Mills   Five miles or so by road from Weymouth but rather nearer by the Dorset Coast Path which passes in front of the inn, Osmington is best known for the view of the Bay, painted by Constable on his honeymoon, and one of his most magnificent pictures. Just over the brow of the hill above the trees on the far right of the picture is one of the county's more unusual residences at Bran Point, a former World War 2 pillbox. There is a precipitous slipway at Osmington used by the lobster catchers, but there are also rocks off Bran and Frenchman's Ledges ready to trap the unwary sailor. The derivation of the inn's name and that of Frenchman's Ledge hardly needs explanation for this was great smuggling territory. The smuggler in question was one Pierre Latour who is said to have used the 16th century inn as his headquarters 200 years ago.

44

Weymouth Harbour The association between Weymouth and the Channel Islands is long, although there are also regular Sealink sailings to Cherbourg, which is actually nearer. One of the sights of the town is the Boat Train easing its way between the parked cars and past the boatyards, warehouses, shops, restaurants, pubs and boarding houses on its journey through the streets to the Quay. There is not much other commercial traffic at Weymouth, although the Bay is a frequent refuge for ships sheltering from Channel storms, but there has been a fishing fleet here for centuries. This century has seen an enormous growth in pleasure craft and Weymouth has become a yachting centre and a venue for international meetings.

The Jubilee Clock, Weymouth Erected for Queen Victoria's Golden Jubilee it has just been repainted in its garishly glorious original colours. Set on the centre of the promenade and overlooking the great sweep of the bay, the clock is a perfect representative of late 19th century Weymouth, a period when the resort was reaching its zenith as a watering place. Weymouth has a longer history than most English resorts, the hotels behind the clock are late Georgian and there is much in the town which is older again, particularly around the harbour. Weymouth has continued to grow through the 20th century, one of the most recent developments being an extension to the harbour to cater for the growing holiday traffic to France and the Channel Islands. One of the unique features of the beach is a remarkable sand sculptor and such old fashioned delights as the punch and judy still attract appreciative crowds.

48

The Isle of Portland This view looks down on the terraces of Fortuneswell, the largest community on the Isle of Portland. Portland, jutting out from Weymouth into the English Channel is joined to the mainland by the thin strip of Chesil Beach. A combination of high tides and fierce storms cuts it off for a few days most winters, and it is to all intents and purposes a piece of solid rock surrounded by the sea.

Stretching away in the distance past the Royal Navy helicopter base and oil storage tanks the Chesil Beach points to West Bay, the downs and Devon. Chesil Beach has been described as 'one of the geological wonders of the world'. More than 15 miles long it is made up chiefly of round flint pebbles with a little quartzite and, at the Portland end, limestone pebbles. The most extraordinary feature of Chesil Beach is that the pebbles are systematically graded throughout its length, the largest at the Portland end, the smallest at Bridport where they are referred to locally as pea gravel. Chesil Beach is a murderous place to contemplate swimming for at all times there is a fierce undertow. Thrilling though the waves are on a stormy day they are best observed at a safe distance.

50

The Lighthouse at Portland Bill Portland stone, said to be the finest in the world, has been used in the construction of buildings as removed in time, distance and purpose as St Paul's Cathedral in London and the United Nations Headquarters in New York. Home of a great naval base and a grim prison, Portland can in some moods seem a grey, storm-swept forbidding place, populated by a self-sufficient breed of fishermen, sailors and quarry workers who have little need of non-islanders. Yet this other worldliness also has great attractions and I have known newcomers settle there instantly and swear it to be the finest place on earth. More than anywhere I know the weather and sea on Portland are everything, their changing moods a constant source of fascination, determining the pattern and rhythm of the lives of the islanders.

52

Upwey Motorists driving along the busy A35 from Dorchester might well assume, as they come over the top of Ridgeway Hill and take in the dramatic view of the bay and the Isle of Portland, that the collection of build-ings immediately beyond the railway bridge is merely the outskirts of Weymouth. In a sense this is correct but it does scant justice to what is also an attractive village with a long history. The little River Wey, which rises close to the barrows above Upwey flows along the tree-lined main street, past the Wishing Well and a succession of handsome houses, mostly built of stone. Upwey has a watermill, and beyond it, further up the road just before it heads up into the bare, bleak downs, is the parish church of St Lawrence. Its tower, prominent in this picture, is of the Perpendicular period, and whilst much of the rest was restored in Victorian times it was well done.

Hardy Statue, Dorchester I sometimes think Thomas Hardy has become the principal industry in Dorset. One day someone will compile a list of all the Hardy tea rooms, plaques on the various buildings featured in his books, sites used by film and TV companies filming Thomas Hardy stories, etc, and a pretty thick volume it will be, although it will need constant updating. This statue of him looking west along the Neolithic trackway which became a Roman road and is today the A31 is set at the main cross roads in the county town of Dorchester, or Casterbridge as Hardy called it. A few hundred yards away is the house, now a bank, where the Mayor of Caster-bridge lived, although when the book was filmed, with Alan Bates in the title role, Corfe Castle was preferred, presumably because Dorchester had changed too greatly since the mid-19th century. Hardy's birthplace is three miles away at Higher Bockhampton and now belongs to the National Trust.

Maiden Castle Some would consider this the greatest pre-historic construction in all England. Due south of Dorchester, it is a series of concentric ditches and ramparts, over a mile in circumference and covering 47 acres. Maiden Castle is able to evoke the past with extraordinary clarity whatever the season, whatever the weather, deserted or crowded with walkers. Just before World War 2 Sir Mortimer Wheeler was in charge of excavations at Maiden Castle (originally Mai Dun or Great Hill) which revealed the graves of 28 Britons killed whilst defending the settlement against the Emperor Vespasian's army which had landed at Radipole on the River Wey some five miles to the south.

St Catherine's Chapel, Abbotsbury This chapel is one of the buildings belonging to the Benedictine abbey of the 11th century, hence the name of the village. The chapel itself dates from the late 14th century and whilst less than 50ft long is notable both for its prominent position and for its state of perfect preservation. St Catherine, incidentally, is the patron saint of spinsters but only those temporarily rather than permanently in such a state it would seem, for a local rhyme asks the Saint's aid in finding a husband, a good one being preferred but any sort being better than none at all. Abbotsbury has been inhabited since Neolithic times, the chief remnants of that period being a hill-fort and 22 round barrows. The Romans are thought to have built fortifications on the site of the fort and in the 18th century a castle was put up there. In 1913 a fire, fanned by a gale blowing in from the sea a mile away destroyed the latter. The finest view of Abbotsbury is to be had from the main road beside the castle site, 705ft high, whence one can see not only the village and the chapel but also Chesil Beach extending some eight miles to Portland.

60

Old Cottages, Abbotsbury The precipitous 1 in 6 descent from the cliff top brings one past the turn for the lush sub-tropical gardens and the beach and into the village. The stone, as can be seen in this view of that part of the main street known as Rodden Row is of a much warmer tone than that found in the Isles of Purbeck and Portland. The double yellow lines painted along the kerbside are a reminder both of the narrowness of the streets and the many visitors which come to Abbotsbury all the year round, almost entirely in their own transport for the railway line is long gone and bus services are minimal.

Mill Pond, Abbotsbury Abbotsbury is still dominated by the monastery and its remains. Throughout the village one comes across gargoyles and other stones from it, and although much of the structure disappeared after the Dissolution there is still plenty to see. The water mill, seen here, is still inhabited although altered, whilst around half of the enormous, 272ft long Abbey Barn is still roofed and thatched. The Abbey House is largely post-Dissolution but the parish church of St Nicholas is earlier, although it is not the one used by the monks; that has all but vanished.

Water has always played a prominent part in the life of Abbotsbury people. The pond not only served the mill but also provided the monks with fish, whilst due south of it a walk through the water meadows leads to the oldest swannery in the world. The swans were once kept by the monks for their meat; today it is open to visitors from late spring until the autumn. Up to 900 swans can be seen, every day in May and June bringing more additions as the cygnets hatch out.

64

Rural Scene near Burton Bradstock A view across the downs looking north. The two main roads which cross this part of Dorset, the A35 from Bridport to Dorchester and the B3157 from Bridport through Burton Bradstock and Abbotsbury to Weymouth offer a series of magnificent vistas, both to the south out across the sea and northwards over the rolling downs. On a clear day it is possible to see from several points along the B3157 the magnificent sweep of Lyme Bay in its entirely from Portland westwards beyond Torbay to Start Point, whilst the A35, first a Neolithic trackway and then a Roman road, is the best possible route for viewing the downs and the many hill forts and barrows.

Burton Bradstock A lovely village of whitewashed, pebble-dashed and stone cottages, once largely inhabited by fishermen, Burton Bradstock is set some half mile back from the sea where the B3157 comes down off the cliffs and levels out on its approach to Bridport. Behind the main road is a network of small lanes, such as this one, centred on the parish church of St Mary, built in the Perpendicular style. It is opposite Burton Bradstock that Chesil Beach begins; eastwards are the chalk downs, westwards the geology changes and becomes much more varied, a prelude to the rich red sandstone of Devon.

68

West Bay A small, neat resort really not much more than a harbour for fishing and pleasure boats at the mouth of the River Brit, a funfair, three pubs and a few other assorted buildings, West Bay is a suburb of Bridport in fact with a shingle beach squeezed between the cliffs. It is much afflicted by fierce winter storms and Dorset County Council is permanently engaged in a fight to preserve the extensive defences erected to keep the English Channel where it belongs. The Great Western Railway extended its Bridport branch down to West Bay in the hope of attracting custom and for a time it did well enough with Sunday school parties and the like, but this was long ago and a road now occupies the old track bed. Herring gulls nest in the yellow Bridport Sand cliffs, atop them to the east is the golf course which extends as far as Freshwater caravan site and the little River Brede which rises at Bridehead, a hamlet north of Abbotsbury.

70

Bridport, seen from the south Bridport is small enough for meadows to reach close to the town centre, and St Mary's is the parish church, which is some way south of the town centre and close to the River Brit. The variety of building materials, an attractive feature of the town, is well shown in this picture, various types of stone, cob (which is chalky mud mixed with straw), brick, plaster, a little timber framing, and on the roofs stone again, tiles, straw and thatch. Although Bridport lost its branch line quite recently it remains an important traffic centre where the roads from Weymouth, Chard, Yeovil and the A31 South Coast trunk road converge.

72

Bridport A town of character Bridport is the only one in Dorset with an industry of national importance. Rope-making has gone on in the town for centuries and has shaped its appearance for its wide pavements were used as rope walks for drying the twine. Rope making still goes on although the locally grown flax has been replaced by man-made fibres. A superb evocation of the history of rope-making, based on the story of a local boy who was hanged for rick-burning in the early 19th century, was produced in 1982 by Anne Jellicoe and shown on television, the cast consisting of over a hundred local people and starring a present-day rope-maker.

There is an excellent museum in South Street containing some of the old rope-making machinery. The Town Hall, seen here at the crossroads in the town centre with a glimpse of the downs beyond, is almost exactly 200 years old having been completed in 1786; the decorative cupola and clock were added in the early 1800s.

The Golden Gap near Chideock Some four miles east of Lyme Regis and three miles west of Bridport, the Golden Gap estate was bought by the National Trust, largely from 'Enterprise Neptune' funds. Seen here in early spring, the gorse a riot of yellow following a mild winter, Golden Gap at 619ft is the highest cliff on all of the south coast of England. There is no better area in the country for finding dinosaur fossils than the Dorset beaches. One of the most famous was the ichthyosaurus discovered by a 12-year old girl below Golden Gap in 1811.

Lyme Regis A town that has for long attracted visitors, Lyme Regis is noted chiefly for its delightful setting up and down the valley of the little River Lim and above and beneath the surrounding cliffs. But if one adds to this a fame thrust on it by two immensely popular writers — neither of them Thomas Hardy! — then it is easy to understand what has of late become its world-wide popularity. Jane Austen visited, danced in, and above all wrote about Lyme in such a way that her name and the town's sometimes seem to be inseparable. And then in our own time John Fowles, who lives in Lyme Regis, set the *French Lieutenant's Woman* here. When this was turned into an Oscar-winning picture with Jeremy Irons and the enigmatic Meryl Streep in the title role and was fetchingly filmed on the Ware Cliffs on the west side of the town the flow of visitors became almost a stampede. Both writers have featured the Cobb, the 600ft long stone breakwater which protects the harbour seen here; indeed it appeared in the poster for the John Fowles film, tens of thousands of copies of which were distributed world-wide — free publicity on a scale beyond the wildest imaginings of the most ambitious tourist office.

Beaminster Set deep amongst the downs in the hinterland of West Dorset, Beaminster has a secluded, almost mysterious air. The memorial seen here in the centre of the triangular shaped market place is relatively modern, dating from 1906 despite its look of centuries old permanence. It commemorates Elizabeth Julia Robinson who lived at Parnham, the great house a mile south of Beaminster. Although you would never guess from the air of tranquility which enfolds its mellow sandstone buildings the town has on at least three occasions suffered severely from fire, and in 1651 seven years after Prince Rupert burned it during the Civil War it was described as 'a collection of blackened, ivy covered ruins'. One building which survived both the 17th century fires and that of 1781 is the parish church of St Mary. The oldest parts, the north wall of the nave, go back to the 13th century, but its great glory is its golden brown 16th century tower, the top of which can be seen here. Superbly proportioned it is decorated with an exuberant collection of statues, gargoyles and pinnacles.

80

Parnham, near Beaminster Parnham is one of the most magnificent of Dorset's many stately homes. As this picture of the east front shows it is essentially Tudor, although there have been many additions and alterations since its complete rebuilding around 1550. Situated one mile south of Beaminster on the Bridport road amidst sloping parkland it was built by Robert Strode, considerably enlarged by Nash in the early 19th century and restored just before World War 1. The formal gardens, fountains and cascades, and terraces populated by peacocks, were laid out between 1910 and 1914. The son of the family which owned it during World War 1, William Rhodes-Moorhouse, died whilst serving in the Royal Flying Corps and was posthumously awarded the Victoria Cross. By a tragic coincidence his son was killed in the Battle of Britain and both are buried on a hill overlooking Parnham.

Today the great house has become celebrated as the home of the School of Craftsmen in Wood, founded in 1977 by John Makepeace. Makepeace has been described as 'The finest craftsman and designer of furniture in wood today' and it is no idle boast. The school, which is a non-profit making educational charity, is not open to visitors but the workshops and the house and gardens are open on Sundays, Wednesdays and public holidays from April to October.

Sherborne School from the tower of Sherborne Abbey The ancient public school, set in the heart of the town and physically joined to the abbey, can trace its origins back to St Aldhelm, one of its earliest scholars being King Alfred. It was substantially developed in the 19th century by its celebrated headmaster, the Rev H. B. Harper and nowadays has about 600 pupils. Sherborne's castle is now no more than a ruin, but its successor, a handsome manor house on the eastern edge of the town remains. Its most famous occupant was Sir Walter Raleigh and is said to be the setting for that historical incident greatly favoured by schoolboys featuring Sir Walter innocently smoking the tobacco he had just introduced to the country, a bucket of water and a distraught servant.

84

Sherborne Abbey Originally a cathedral and for 370 years the see of the Bishop of Wessex, this massive church became monastic in 998AD remaining part of the Abbey until the Dissolution, in 1539. It was then sold to the town — for £230! — and the existing parish church was demolished. The abbey was however kept intact and has been maintained by the town's people ever since. The south view of the church is in the Perpendicular style dating from c1430. There was a major fire in 1437 resulting from a quarrel between the monks and the townspeople and its traces can still be seen in the Abbey to this day. Restored extensively — and inevitably — in the 1850s, Selbourne Abbey is currently undergoing further repair.

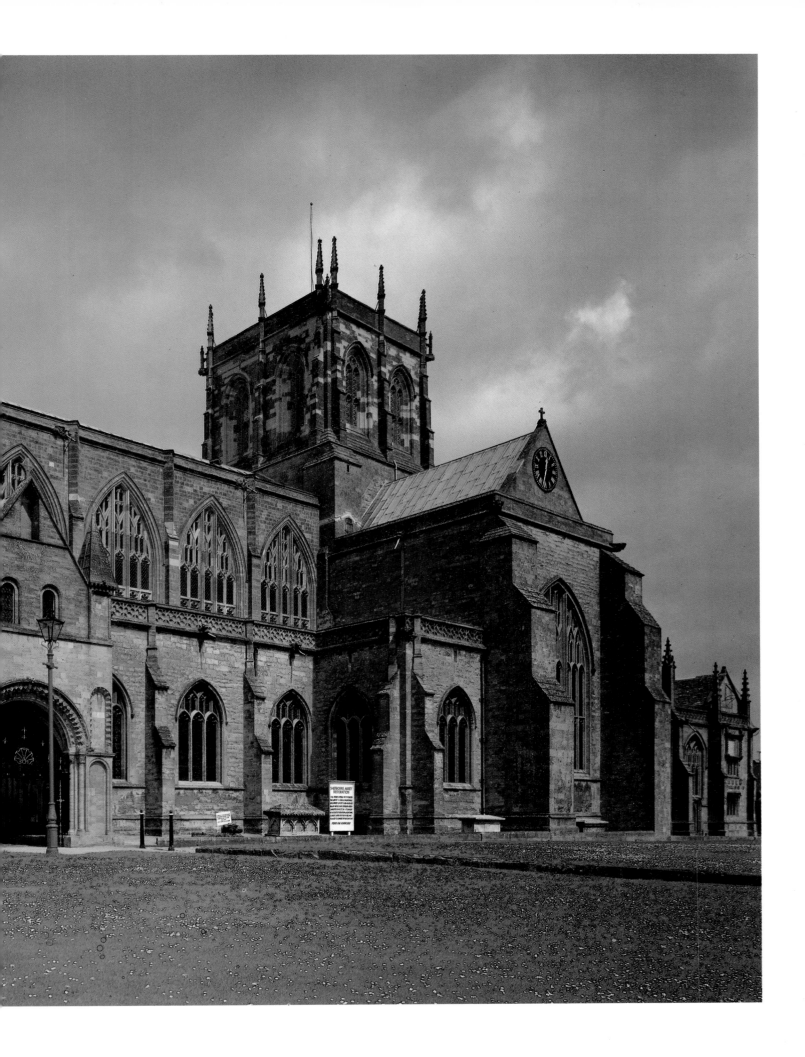

88

Cerne Abbas This is one of the show villages of Dorset. Its most famous feature is the great, naked, club-carrying giant, dating back no one can say how far but almost certainly at least 2,000 years, carved in chalk immediately to the north of the village. Cerne was once rather more than a village with its Benedictine abbey founded in the late 9th century, and for centuries was a commercial centre taking advantage of its position in the Cerne Valley midway between Sherborne and Dorchester. But when the railway came it passed along the next valley to the west,

Maiden Newton became the junction for Bridport and prospered whilst Cerne Abbas declined.

The motor car exposed Cerne's picturesqueness and brought about its revival. The perpendicular tower of St Mary's parish church dates from the days of the abbey. It is a pleasant walk along Abbey Street, past the church and the handsome timber-fronted terrace — a rare feature in Dorset — through the Abbey farm and the graveyard where the abbey church once stood, and on up the hill to stand atop and look down on the Giant and the village.

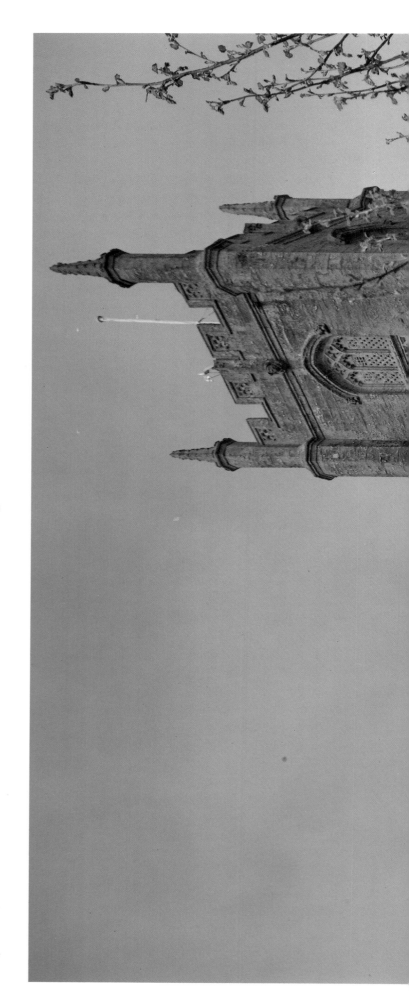

Bluebells near Puddletown The stony soil of the south-east of the county, combined with offshore winds means that the land, where it is not heathland, is principally given over to pasture and trees are relatively sparse and fairly stunted in growth. But further inland in more sheltered conditions, and where the soil is richer there are extensive woodlands. The valley of the little river Piddle which rises in the downs east of Cerne Abbas and runs to Poole Harbour has a wealth of delightfully named villages like Piddletrenthide, Piddlehinton and Affpudle. In spring it glows with the purples and blues of rhododendrons and bluebells.

90

Athelhampton House near Puddletown
Athelhampton House is one of the finest stately homes in Dorset and one of the oldest in the country. Situated on the main A35 between Puddletown and Tolpuddle and some six miles from Dorchester, the house stands on a site that has been in use since at least the 13th century when the Martin family took it over. The present house dates from 1504 when Sir William Martin, who had been Lord Mayor of London in 1493, had it constructed very much in the form we presently see it. Although there have been additions since that time enough of it, particularly the great hall, is early Tudor for it to be accurately described as a fine and rare example of that period. Athelhampton House is still a home but is open on occasions to the general public.

92

Tolpuddle A pleasant though not excessively picturesque village Tolpuddle lies on the A35 Poole to Dorchester road, some six miles east of the latter. Once a year the national media descends upon it for the great parade and rally attended by past and, sometimes, present cabinet and prime minsters held to commemorate the Tolpuddle Martyrs. In 1834 a group of agricultural labourers met in the village to form a union as part of Robert Owen's Grand National Consolidated Trades Union.

Such an act was seen by many landowners as a direct threat to their position of privilege and the Tolpuddle men were prosecuted for taking an 'unlawful oath'. They were found guilty and transported to Australia. The furore this produced throughout the land brought about the quashing of their sentence two years later, and the Tolpuddle incident is generally regarded as the true beginning of the trade union movement in Britain.

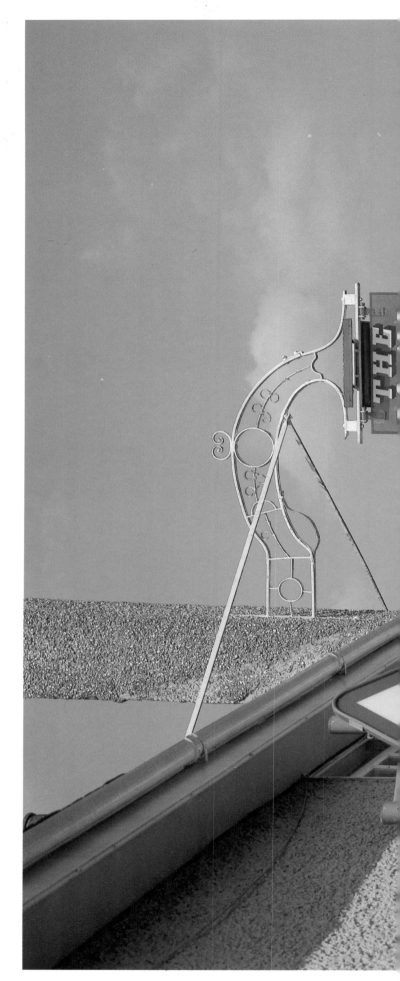

Milborne St Andrew A village on the Dorchester to Blandford road. Milborne St Andrew's school sign is a reminder that in a county as rural as Dorset there are many villages fighting to keep their local schools. The arguments rage fiercely. Often village life seems to revolve around the church, the shop and the school. In many villages the shop and the school are under threat, usually on economic grounds, but sometimes it is social and educational ones which threaten the latter.

In some of the more remote parts of the north of the county there are children who live a life little less secluded than that of their Victorian great-great grandparents. Their mothers and fathers may be almost totally occupied running the farm, and the children will see few others to communicate with in a one or two teacher school of perhaps no more than 15 to 20 pupils of a wide range of ages. This social and educational deprivation has to be balanced against the undesirability of small children travelling considerable distances to school, and the loss to the village if the school is closed down. It is never an easy decision.

Milton Abbas A rather extraordinary place, Milton Abbas is the result of the antics of the megalomaniac, though hardly unique, Earl of Dorchester. Between 1771 and 1790 he destroyed the old market town alongside the site of Milton Abbey, founded in 935AD by King Athelstan, in order than he might build himself a bigger and better mansion than the one he already had. To give Lord Dorchester his due he built a new village — out of his sight — and it would seem the old town had known better days. The two cottages seen here are typical of those Lord Dorchester had built around 1780. They are identical, neatly whitewashed with their thatched roofs, set amongst the grass, step by step down the hill, as pretty as a picture. The layout of the village was designed by none other than Lancelot 'Capability' Brown for which John Newman records he was paid £105.

Blandford Forum A sign beside the bridge where the A354 from Dorchester passes over the River Stour at the western approach to the town announces that Blandford is 'an interesting Georgian town'. This has always struck me as a somewhat half-hearted description — what town doesn't contain something of interest? Blandford is a distinctly handsome place, full of Georgian buildings, one of the finest being the parish church of St Peter and St Paul, seen here, dating from 1733-9. As its name indicates Blandford is of Roman origin but a fire in 1731 destroyed its centre. Disastrous as this was for the inhabitants its immediate rebuilding resulted in a pleasing unity of style. Blandford was once the centre of the Dorset button-making industry but this largely died out in the early years of the present century. Its inhabitants still depend to a large extent for their livelihood on agriculture — or the army for there is a large camp just outside the town on the Salisbury road. The 'Great Working of Steam Engines' held each September up above Blandford on the top Shaftesbury road is a marvellous and comprehensive — if sometimes muddy — celebration of farming and the rural way of life of days gone by.

Okeford Fitzpaine As this view demonstrates, Okeford Fitzpaine is a village where buildings and nature blend with an especial harmony, despite or perhaps because of the variety of flint, stone and brick, as well as half-timbering used in the construction of the houses and cottages over the years. Time has mellowed textures and colours although the inhabitants' pride in their village ensures that paintwork is always bright, and the rich soil produces a riot of blooms in the gardens and hedgerows in and about the village. Indeed all the villages in the greensand vale south of Sturminster Newton and beneath the chalk ridge are glorious with flowers.

102

Sturminster Newton Sturminster and Newton were once two separate communities, facing each other on opposite banks of the River Stour, which rises over the Somerset border in the Blackmoor Vale and flows into the sea at Christchurch. The six arch bridge has long united them into one quite small, but quite important town. The Romans were here and the Saxons built a castle. All that remains of this is a grass mound and pieces of broken masonry. It has been suggested that the mound originated as an Iron Age fort. Once almost every Dorset town held a cattle market but as transport has become easier so these have declined in number, the remaining ones increasing in size and importance. Although Sturminster Newton lost its railway nearly 20 years ago when the picturesque but roundabout and underused Somerset and Dorset line closed down, its position in the heart of the relatively sparsely populated, richly agricultural north of the county ensured the survival of its livestock market and today it is the most important in the whole of Dorset.

Shaftesbury Although in places Shaftesbury has a somewhat shabby, neglected air it also possesses many ancient and picturesque buildings. This surely is one of the best known views in all England, looking down the steep slope of the cobbled Gold Hill, above the myriad shades of brown and red of the tiled and thatched cottages to the rolling meadows and copses stretching away to the distant Blackmore Vale.

Shaftesbury is undoubtedly historic — the Romans built a temple, King Alfred founded an abbey, the dead boy king, Edward V was buried here after his murder at Corfe, Canute died here and Robert Bruce's queen was held a prisoner. There are those who would argue that not much has happened in Shaftesbury since — no railway contemplated the 700ft climb to reach it, but in fact it is an important cross roads where the London to Exeter A30 and the Poole and Bournemouth to Bath and Bristol A350 meet.

Witchampton A village off the beaten track, Witchampton was once much more in the mainstream of Dorset affairs. The Iron Age road, later developed by the Romans, from Old Sarum to Badbury Rings and Dorchester ran through it. You would hardly guess so today for the lane which links Witchampton with the outside world meanders in a most unpurposeful way through the village before gaining the Wimborne-Cranborne road. A Roman villa of considerable magnificence was unearthed early in the 19th century to the west of Witchampton, various of its treasures being presently on display in the Dorchester and British Museums. Apart from the many pretty houses and cottages such as the one pictured here with its carefully tended gardens, Witchampton possesses the ruins of a manor house and tithe barn, a church dedicated to St Mary and St Cuthbega, and a large paper mill.

Badbury Rings Dorset is particularly rich in prehistoric relics, a result of the settlement by Neolithic men along the hilltops. Badbury Rings, along with Maiden Castle, is the best known of them all. A great Iron Age fort to the north of the Wimborne-Blandford road, the Rings are visited by some 200,000 people annually, a good many of them school parties who love to run up and down the extensive slopes. Part of the Bankes Estate, Badbury Rings are now the property of the National Trust. Much excavation remains to be done to establish the date and history of the Rings, and the National Trust is also deciding how best to prevent further erosion and to provide information for visitors which up to now has been lacking.

110

Index

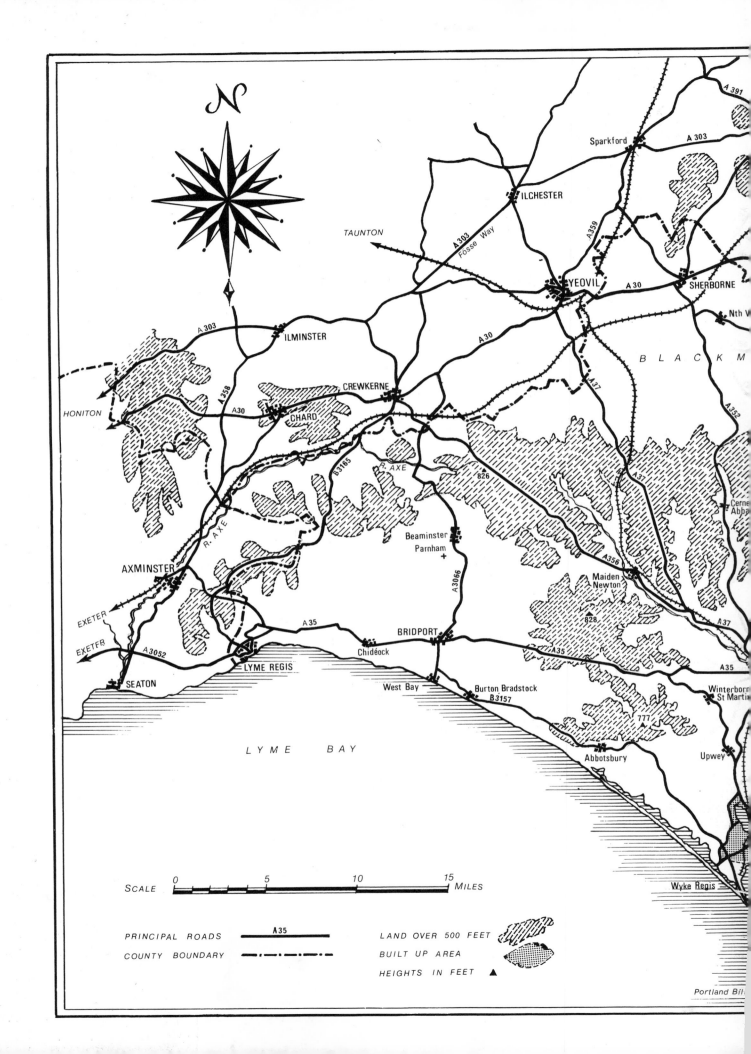

N

SCALE 0   5   10   15   MILES

PRINCIPAL ROADS ———— A35 ————

COUNTY BOUNDARY ·—··—··—··—··—··—·

LAND OVER 500 FEET

BUILT UP AREA

HEIGHTS IN FEET ▲